ella zelensky

At First Light

Ella Zelensky

at first light

ella zelensky

also by ella zelensky

Divine Decree

Little Dreamer

© Ella Zelensky, 2023. All Rights Reserved

at first light

ella zelensky

younger me
was as little
as i am
with gentle touch
and watchful eyes
younger me
wrote poems
to survive her
struggle too
younger me is
unaware that
i exist
younger me
thought she
would die
now, older me is here
living and breathing

-       and writing a beautiful book about it

at first light

ella zelensky

chapter one:
struggling

sometimes people
turn out to be
a lesson
not a friend

if i could
i would walk
across the ocean
at night on days
i was upset until
i was standing right
in the middle of it
feel water
entwine with sky
and be surrounded
by the illusion of
standing among
the stars

at first light

how did such
a beautiful
and close friendship
turn to sand

ella zelensky

you cannot stay
for the one
who does not

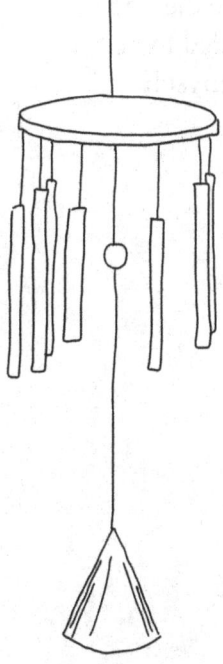

at first light

i was desperate
for the ones who
did not want me
but not desperate
to be the one i
needed to be
for myself

i grieve over memories
that don't exist

at first light

if they don't
quite leave
they can claim
why they couldn't
always stay

just because you're
one of their first options
doesn't change the fact
that you are one

you must be empty inside
for your apology to be too

i was so preoccupied
with how you could
learn to treat me
in the future
that i excused how
you did in the present

i'm tired of yelling at myself
from the inside

ella zelensky

i unravel so quickly i border
lack of consciousness
but my eyes stay slightly open
i'm like a flag whipping in the wind
a baby bird whose wings are
convulsing violently
as it falls from the sky

at first light

where were you
when i needed
you most
why did you not
hold my hand
or look me in the eye
or hug me to life
when i thought
i would die

-       asking myself

i can't keep up
this game of
hide and seek
from myself

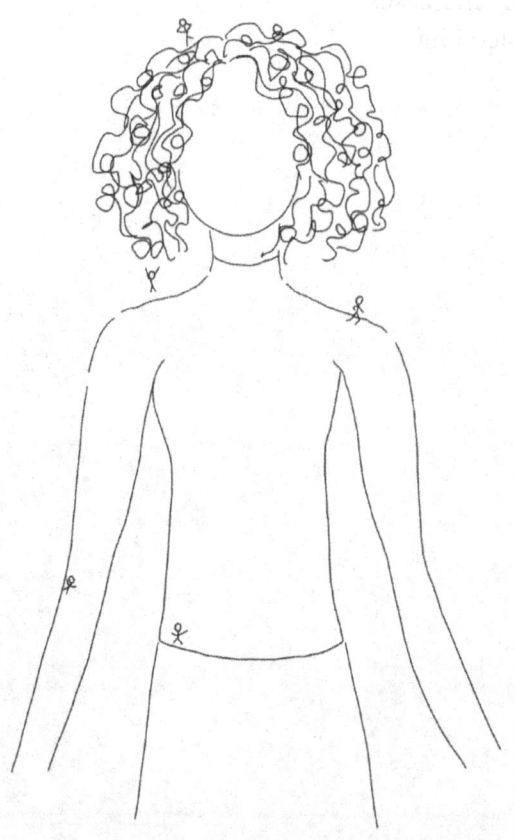

at first light

you used to heal
my bleeding heart
but now
when you press
your hand
against it
it doesn't heal
it only increases
the bleeding

i felt like
the friendship
was a scam
people really
are good at
advertising
themselves

at first light

later in life
when the truth
of her suffering
finally occurred
to her
she was
beside herself
for not being
beside herself
all those years

my heart screamed
so hard i caused
severe weather
warnings globally

at first light

the monster
ripped her
throat apart
stole her
heart from
her chest
and clawed
her eyes blind
with all her
sanity taken away
she lay on
the ground
staring at stars
she could no
longer see
waiting to die
but never dying

ella zelensky

there is no
life here
nothing grows
it only snows

how strange it is
that so many of us
are so divorced
from the body
we inhabit

ella zelensky

when i exhale
and the bubbles
erupt and rise
i see worlds in them
alternate universes
that could have
been different
bright
beautiful
as they surround me
i reach for them
instead of my real life
and almost die
until i choose not to

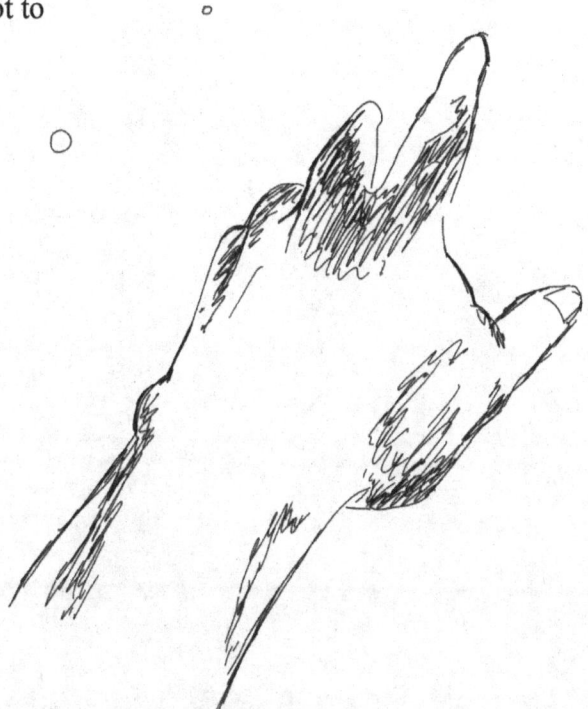

if you were stood
in front of yourself
would you say out loud
what you tell yourself
inside your head

ella zelensky

under light
and dust
she falls
to the centre
of the stage
in a heavy heap
she barely
looks around
barely seeks
any help
just sits there
hunched over
eyes half closed
staring at the floor
no longer human
but robot

they played their
chess aggressively
caring more to
humiliate the opponent
than letting them
realise their potential

don't test me
you wouldn't even be
able to cheat
if you tried

at first light

only someone
who is numb inside
could inflict such pain
on others without
flinching themselves

sometimes i spend
so much time
missing parts of
my younger self
or trying to envision
parts of my future self
that i forget how
beautiful it would be
to invest my full attention
into the woman i
operate as now
because right now i am
doing remarkable things
that don't deserve to
be treated as nothing

at first light

when i escape the
chamber of my brain
i quickly resort to
building another like it
all i want is space
and yet i negate it
every time by making less

within everyone is
someone hidden who is
contemplating extensively
questioning carefully
hurting deeply
and yearning secretly

our hands have a habit
of holding one another
in times of sadness
it shows that we are
there for ourselves
before we even realise

when you are finally
walking under the sun
which will you choose
fearing your shadow
or appreciating the light

at first light

it feels good
to leave the end
of the tunnel
and see the world
and all its
brightness
colours
and warmth envelop
you once again

as i cried in the garden
on the verge of hopelessness
the tears that fell from my eyes
began to grow flowers

there's a difference
between denying
your strength and
not having any left

i must remember that writing
is not
to fill the empty pages of a
book
but to fill the empty soul

i have nothing more
to say to you
but rest assured
i have plenty to
write about

ella zelensky

at first light

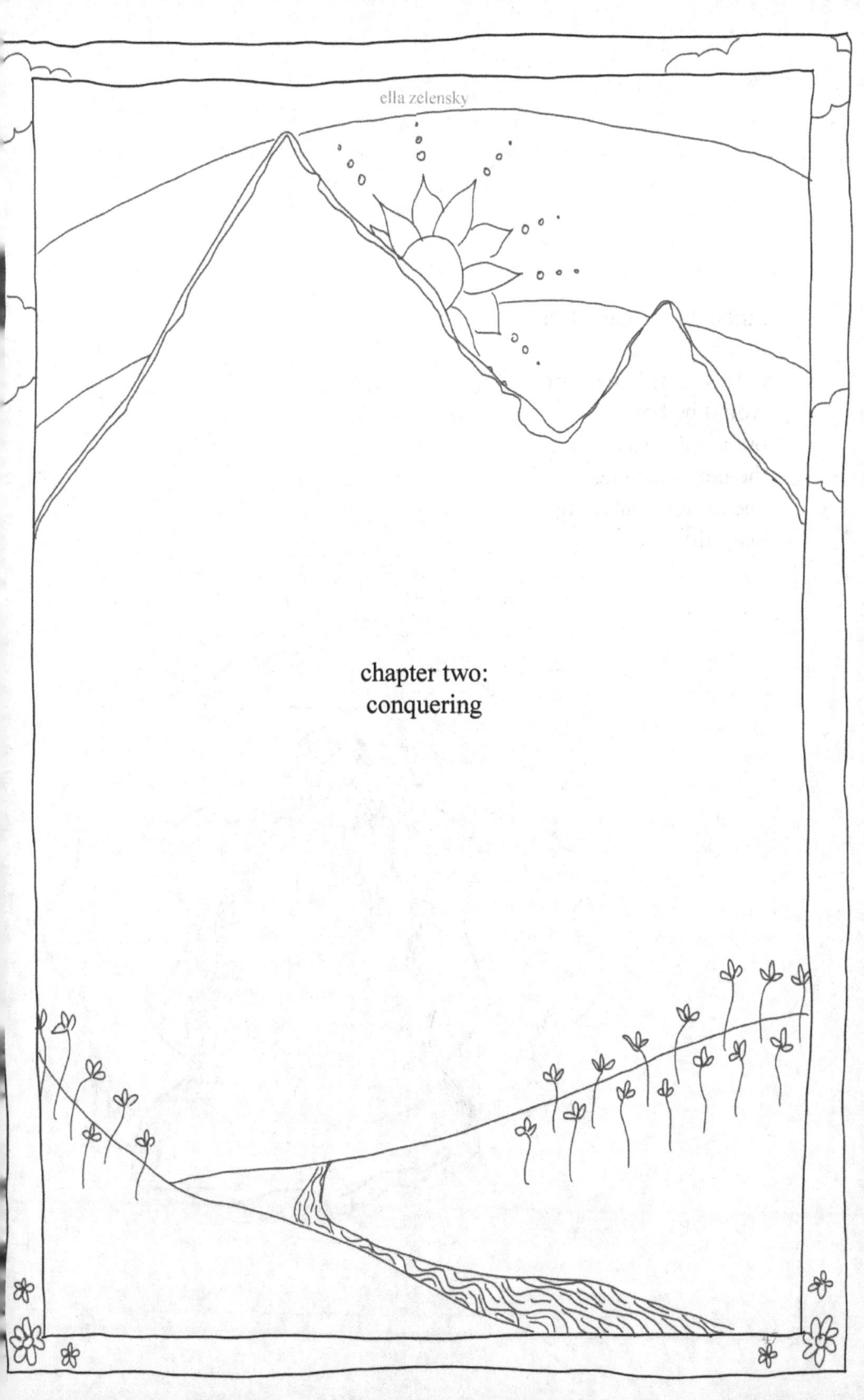

i thought so many times
that not being
in this world anymore
would be better
but would wake up
the next morning
and notice something
beautiful

my eyes take on
a new shape
hauntingly clear
when my survival mode
shatters the door
in front of me

when one knows
who they are
their eye contact
alone
will confront people

ella zelensky

if you throw me
into water
i can breathe
if you push me
into fire
i emerge unscathed
kick me off
the precipice and
i fly
nothing you do now
will kill me off

i walked into
that toilet stall
a girl devoid
of life
and walked out
with the rage
of humanity's
voices in me

she stood in her independence
before they even had the chance
to leave her out

you thought you
could do it again
but the arrows
you fired at me
were ones
you could never
survive yourself

ella zelensky

when i awaken in
the theatre
rays of light from
the windows high above
crown my head and
illuminate my eyelashes
i slowly raise my hands
turning them as i realise
that i am not dead
i am not gone
i am here
i am alive

at first light

this pain that used to consume me
now transforms me into a victor
not a victim

ella zelensky

the mistake we make is
confusing trauma with identity
working past your trauma doesn't
mean you have lost your identity
what it actually means is refusing
to allow an inner narrative to
dictate your worth and growth

at first light

you think
you have
won and
that is
your greatest
loss

ella zelensky

the coalescing
of every adversity
you have overcome
has made you
more prepared
than ever
to defeat your
next obstacle

the stairs you
are walking up
were built by you

ella zelensky

if i walk back
at halfway
it will take as long
to reverse my progress
as it will to complete it
so it would only make
sense to finish
what i started
to climb the mountain
i know i can

powerful, the little one

a lantern burns
within me
do you not
realise the more
damage you
create in me
the more my light
will beam through

at first light

when we realise that we
possess all that we need
we realise how much less
others possessed all that
we wanted

ella zelensky

i see her
over there
i have found
her once more
i am running
back to myself

you sit comfortably
in your chair
whilst i am stood up
that is the difference
between you and me
you are too afraid
to raise from your
comfort and security
whereas i am the one
standing for something

ella zelensky

you can stand
up for yourself by
standing up and walking away

at first light

you lost me
because i
found myself

ella zelensky

the wave towers
over my body
i cannot run
for i have not
the time to
so i must stand still
i must face this wave
let it rise and fall
as my lungs do
let it crash
swarm over and
past me
until the water
lowers
and only i remain

each and
every one
of your tears
are your
body's way
of keeping count
not losing count
of your reasons
to live

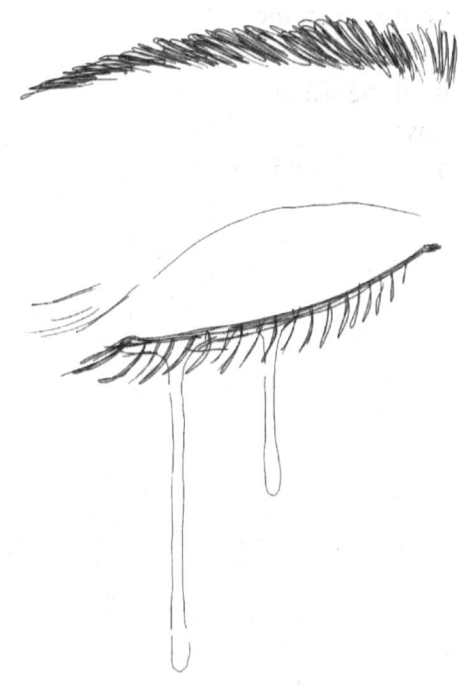

ella zelensky

what doesn't work
out in the way
you wanted
can actually work
out for you in the way
you needed
this is the importance
of not mistaking
a win as a defeat

the way my heartbeat
soldiers on until death
is one of the greatest
motivators i know

ella zelensky

when i fear i
will run out of poems
i remember it is
the quality and not
the quantity of my messages
that carry the ultimate
impact

i can be witty
in my writing
i just fear it will
slice people in two

did you really think i would never say anything?

at first light

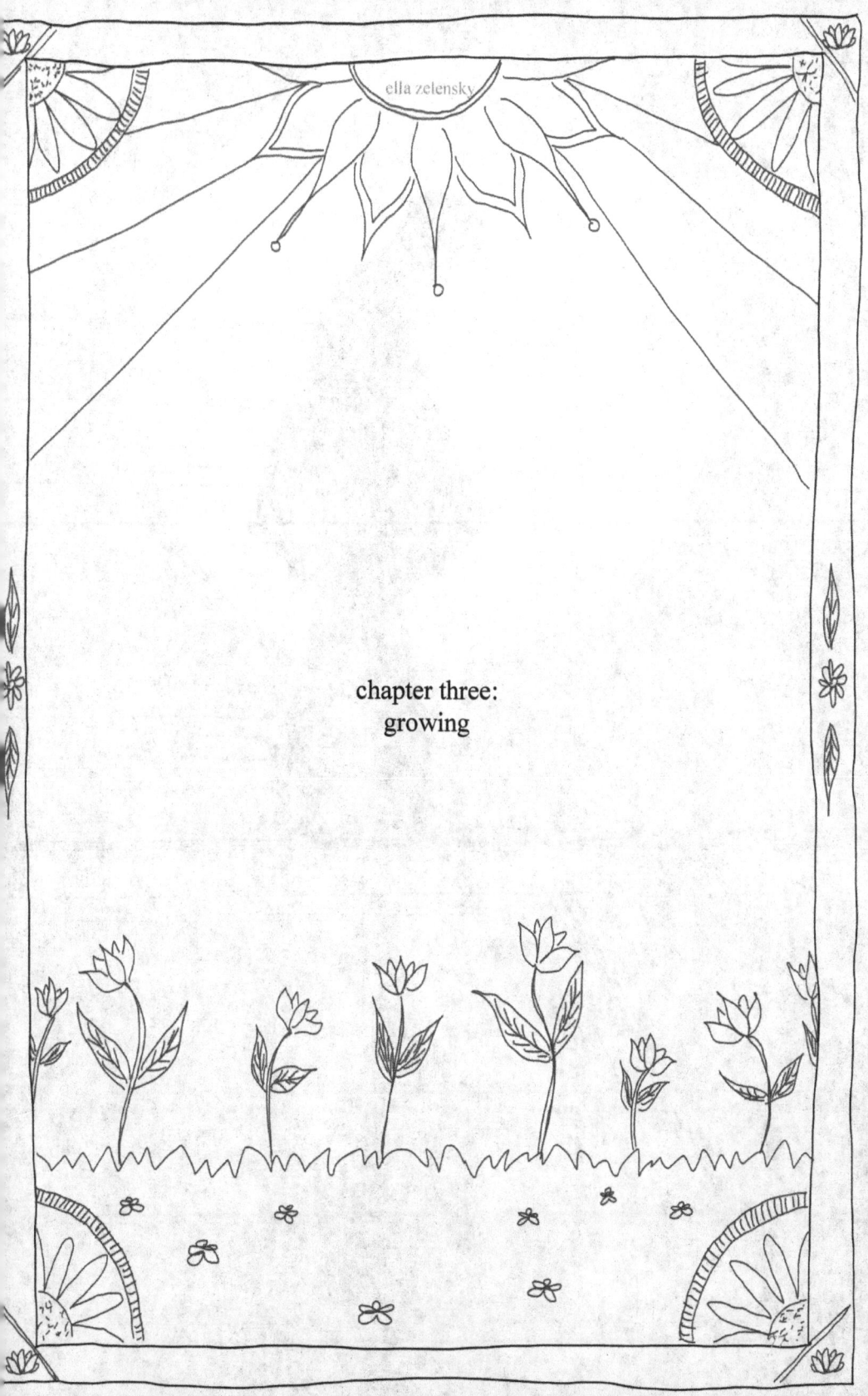

ella zelensky

chapter three:
growing

at first light

people are afraid of the dark
when they haven't figured
out how to be their own light yet

ella zelensky

you rotate faces
when attending
different places
but in doing so
who are you really
trying to hide from

ella zelensky

i don't think
it's crazy to
talk to yourself
not a lot of people
know how to

at first light

i'm not alone
for being left out
they're alone for
frantically gluing
themselves
to people as soon
as they walk into
the room

it's funny how we continue
to ask people all around town
for directions on how to
find ourselves

if it makes you
indistinguishable
from those around you
it isn't solidarity
it's rationalised uniformity

ella zelensky

there is no polite way
of telling somebody
to be untrue to themselves

some people
when handed
a crown of thorns
will care not
for the prick of
the thorn so much
as they desire
the title of the crown

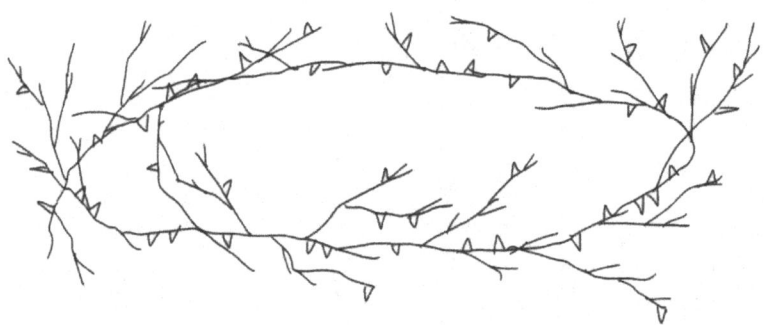

ella zelensky

someone could throw
a whole bucket full of
water and ice at them
and they still wouldn't
wake up to the lesson

at first light

those who look
from the inside out
will never understand
what others see
from the outside in
until they
get out of the group
they're in

ella zelensky

you cannot
lay out the
cement and
expect it not
to set

we can't get
enough of it
until we have
had enough of it

ella zelensky

we are told to
run from one
point to another
in a world that is
rapidly shifting
beneath our feet

at first light

nowadays
it's the cliché
and unoriginal
that is successful
we are still
being taught
to throw what
makes all of us
unique out the window

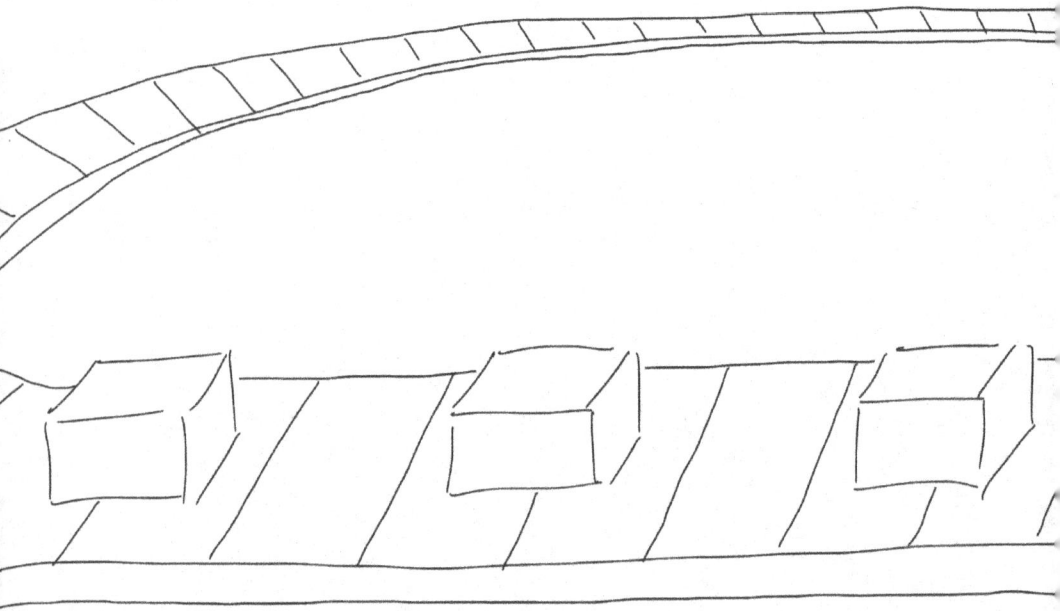

ella zelensky

we measure people's
intelligence based
on tests that don't
highlight their expertise
and draw conclusions
without watching them
thrive in environments
that make evident their
extraordinary abilities

holding in your voice
is like holding in your breath
you'll lose your life
if you continue to do it

if you walk the world on your toes
your feet will begin to bleed

at first light

when you see
it as a competition
you will fear the
potential of losing
but when you see it
as a learning
opportunity
you know you'll
never lose

ella zelensky

they paused
had it gone
differently
they thought
would i have
actually lost
if i had won

at first light

confetti falls
around them
yet they do
not move

ella zelensky

you don't even
need speech
or volume
to speak volumes

at first light

do the unexpected
it teaches us more
than the expected

ella zelensky

i should have
my own permission
to do what is best

you have accepted
their belittling
of you because
it bears familiarity
to the way you
belittle yourself

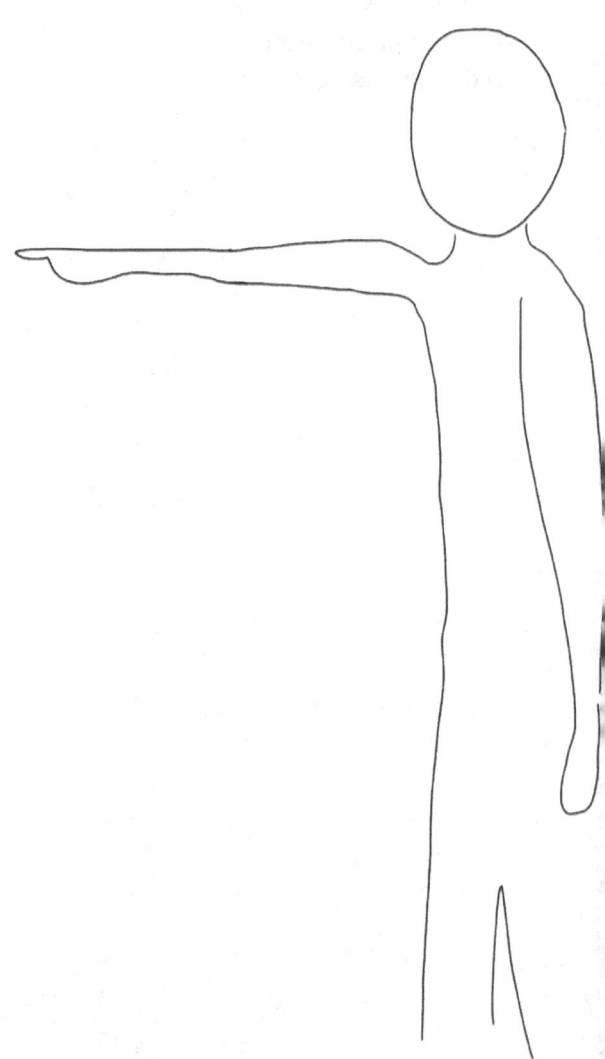

you liked me until i showed you
i had a voice

i continue
to question
their behaviour
as if i don't
already know
the answer

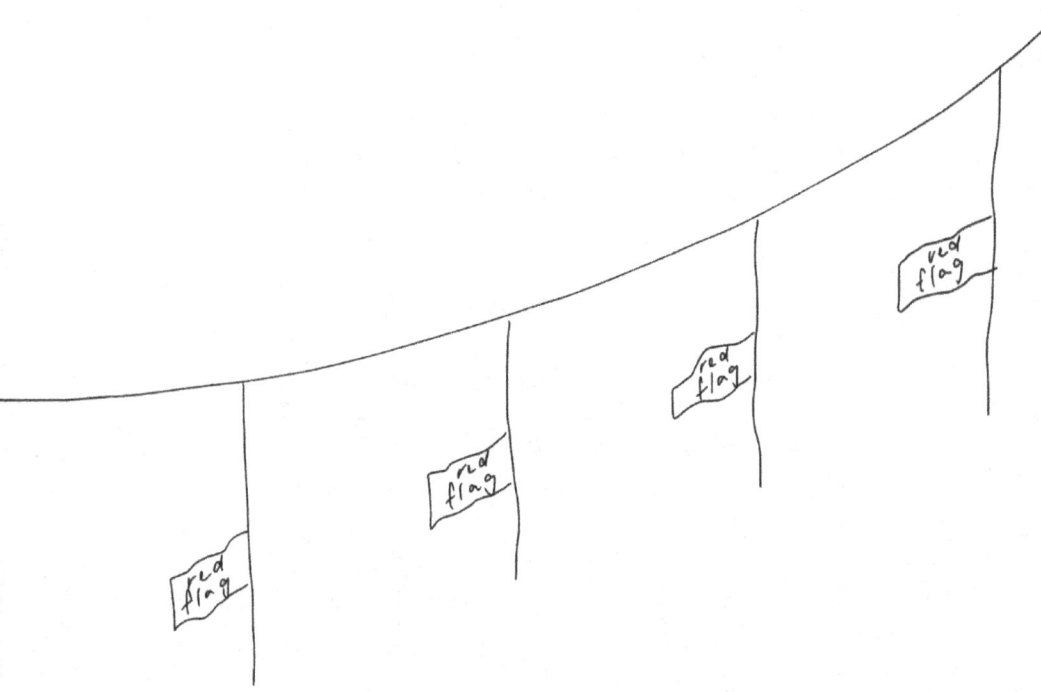

when we were young
we played a game
at school where
four teams had to
steal eggs from
one another's nests
and count how many
more a particular team
obtained than others
i hadn't realised how
deeply HPE games
reflected experiences
of greed
mistrust
competition
exhaustion
self defence
and immorality
in the real world

even if someone says
they are keeping you
safe behind bars
it doesn't change the fact
that you've been kept
in a prison

her tears were like
currency to him

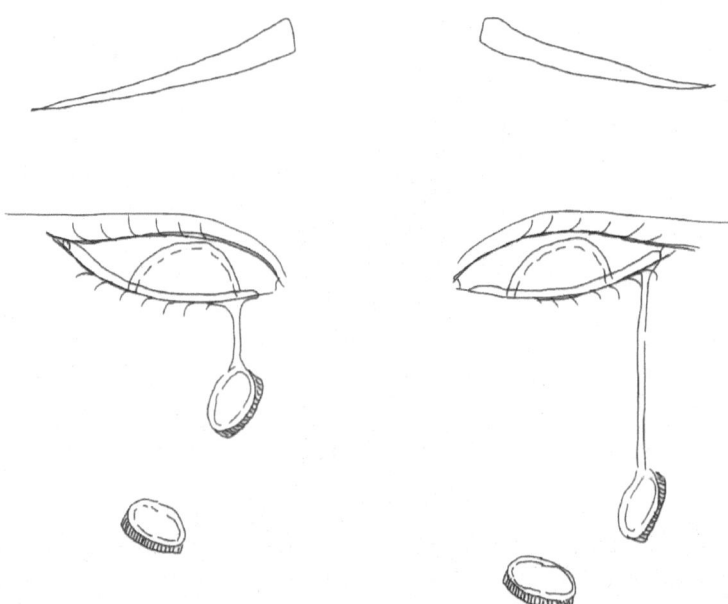

just because they were
there to catch your tears
doesn't downplay
the fact that they
caused them

it's not about them
proving you wrong
they just like the sound
of their own voice

they're counting
on the fact that
you won't realise
your own worth

at first light

do not care
if they unfollow you
or suddenly
distance themselves
how can you
expect them to
follow your journey
when they aren't
even ready to
follow their own

ironically
we desensitise
ourselves
to beating
ourselves up

for some reason
we are awfully attracted
to the perpetuation
of our and others' misery

ella zelensky

having friends
doesn't always
mean they are
real friends
it may be that
your solitude
is your contentment
whilst their
company is
their loneliness

at first light

people that are
laughing at you
will often hide behind
your assumption
that they're laughing
with you

ella zelensky

people will
enter and exit
the chapters
in the book
of your life
what you must
make sure of
however is that
you remain the
author of it

work with the silence
they won't
speak to you
so speak one on one
with yourself
say exactly what you
need to hear
because they don't
deserve to hear
what you have to say

ella zelensky

**you cannot live someone
else's life for them**

don't compromise
your maturity level
if you're attempting to
make someone else
realise their lack
of one

ella zelensky

we spend about a third
of our lives asleep in bed
so we must make sure we don't
spend more of it asleep
in the head

at first light

an echo chamber
is loud and confusing
all the doors are
guarded by its speakers
and no matter how much
you cover your ears
the noise will barge
into your soul and claim
you as another advocate
for a cause you don't
quite comprehend yourself

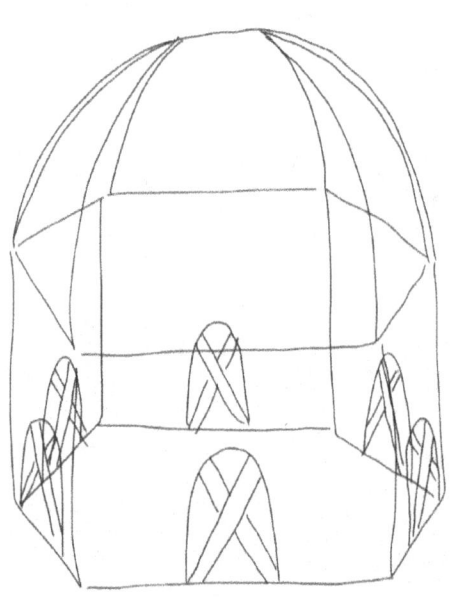

in your quest for knowledge
so too must you be on a
quest to actually want to learn

at first light

it isn't what
we've done wrong
to deserve
a punishment
it's what we've
done right
to earn the
experience

ella zelensky

we give things a go
all the time
so why not this time

where a challenge is given
a capacity isn't taken
but rather improved

sometimes preparation
isn't as beneficial as
being placed in a
sudden situation
to be put on the spot
forces us to make
smart decisions
even preparation
can't predict

are you sure you are
prepared to navigate
life without knowing
or being who you are

training your body is great
but without training
your mind
without sense of
purpose or self
working out will only
be as good as
carving an empty shell

at first light

fragility is beautiful
but be wary of who
is attracted to it
for some will love
the way it teaches
them to be better
whilst others will take
advantage of it to break
and control you

ella zelensky

kindness is free
and yet we still choose
to make others the
cost of our hostility

at first light

when we learn to embrace
maturity and growth
we will fall in love with what
it feels like to be humbled

i shall not deny myself a good life

at first light

stop opening the same door
that leads to a brick wall

if you were given
the ticket
would you
neglect the
experience

- what it means to learn

at first light

at first light

the planets
are preparing
to say farewell
to their long
time friend

ella zelensky

we have learnt
the reaction of
feeling bad
but not the action
of doing good

at first light

it's easy to ignore
the human being
sitting in the corner
but it is a noble thing
to sit with them

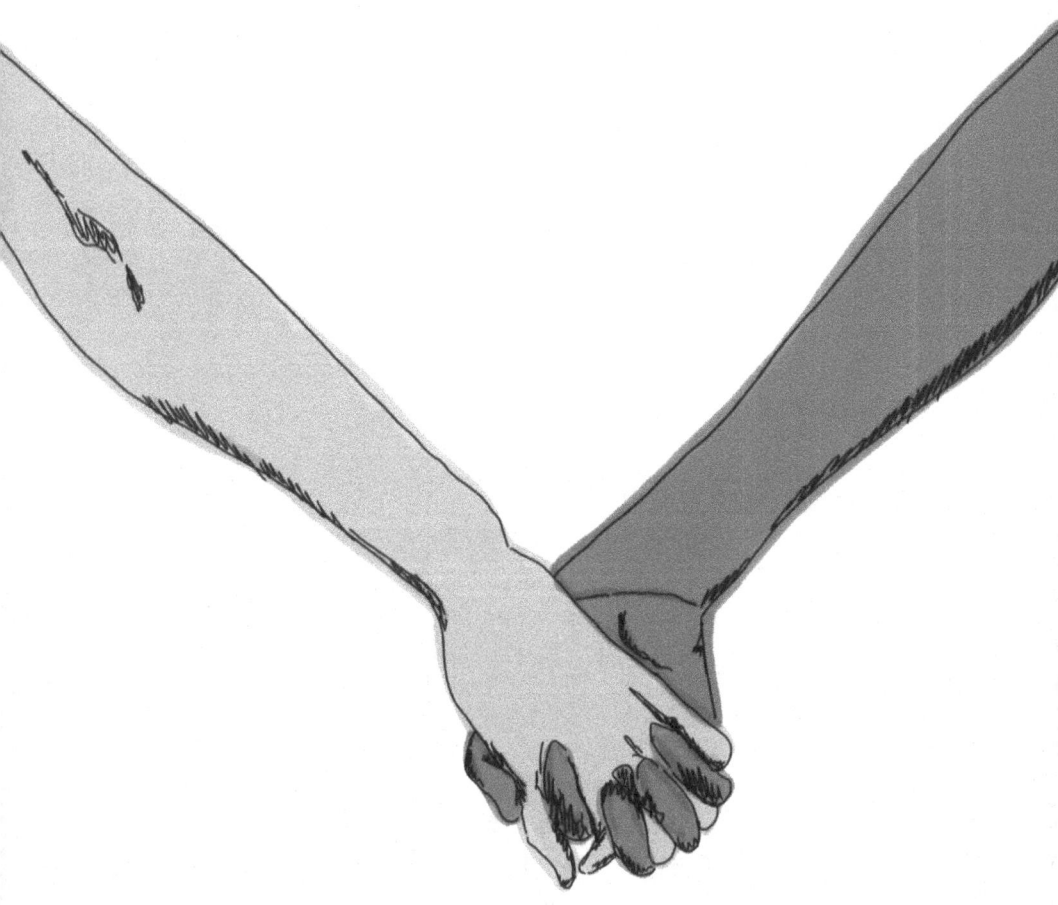

ella zelensky

our plates brim
with the dreams
of starving children
we waste the leftovers
as if they won't
die tonight

it will take lifetimes
of our own
to save theirs
but we must never
ever give up on them

ella zelensky

as the young girl
drank the water
from her cup
she wondered
how many cups
it would take to
hold the world's
tears
in wonder
she stared at the
sombre scene
in front of her
and saw the eyes of
other children staring
back into hers
with the same level
same intensity of
inquisitiveness

at first light

he wanted to cry
but knew he had to be
a strong little boy
so he kept carrying
the buckets

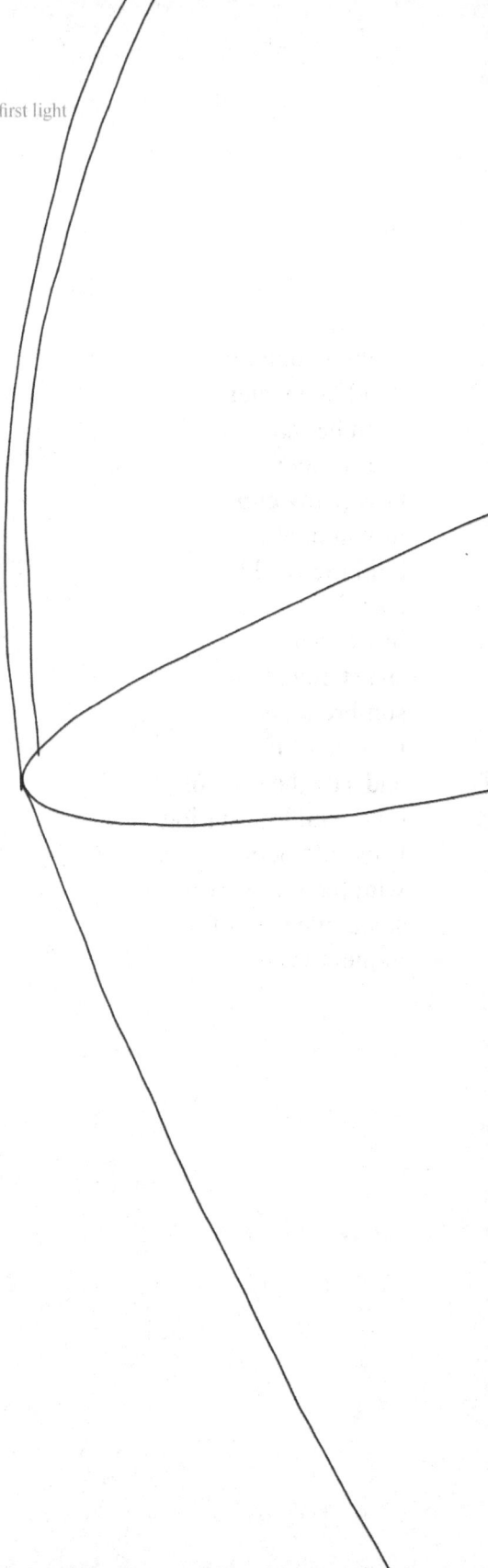

ella zelensky

she sits in a cage
in tears
accepting that
she will never
be allowed to leave
she hears men outside
arguing loudly over her
and how much they're
willing to pay
she is learning fast
that she is both
valuable and worthless
and most of all
helpless

you spoke to her
but she heard the voices
of two

- intergenerational brainwashing

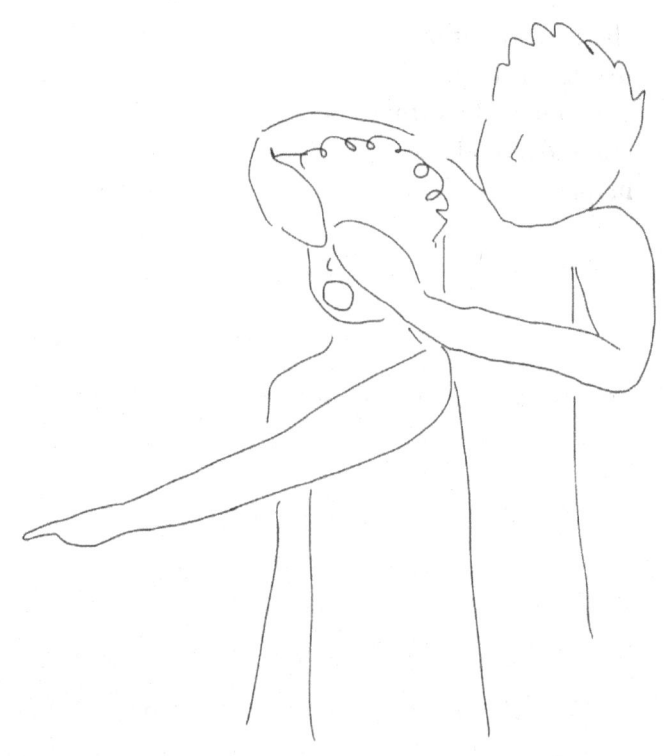

ella zelensky

as he threw her
into the grave
as did he of himself
both were to die
but their afterlife
that would differ
tremendously

at first light

what is a son
who ensures
name and pride
when men act
like god and throw
god's creation aside

- family legacy

ella zelensky

oh how the boy's
mother wept
at the thought of her son
fighting and crying
before drowning
in the lake
before she resented
the water
in her mind came the image
of her womb
the place she carried
him not long ago
it too held water
except he was asleep
in there peacefully
not thrashing around
not fighting it
just laying still
and happy in his
mother's loving presence

in those different parts
of the same world
she is a mother too

ella zelensky

the teacher
becomes a mother
of an entire
classroom as
she scrambles up
in front of
her small students
spreads out her arms
and turns herself
into a shield
for their sake

they tell them
to stay on the boat
the students
trust their instruction
until they do not
removing their shoes
and ordering them in the
corner of the room
accepting that they
will drown together as
the boat fills with water

ella zelensky

life jackets
litter the beach
and people
dare to regard
those who once
wore them
as an inconvenience
to the world

at first light

how can they stand out in the world
when they don't even fit into it

ella zelensky

brave are
the immigrants
who move from
nothing to
nothing
in order to
build everything

they live as
a pile of bones
not dead
but not
alive either

ella zelensky

the independence
we fought for
flows through
our veins
we are small
but mighty
you will hear the
crowds of our nation
chanting with
passionate emotion
from oceans away

at first light

as a child i could feel
lessons flowing through my veins
that my immigrant father
hadn't taught me yet

ella zelensky

at night
the two children
illuminate
their tent
with a flashlight
giggling despite
the hurting of
their hearts
as if their situation
won't consume them
it is their little
illuminated tent
that serves
as a lantern of hope
for their community
and for the world

at first light

when i looked
into their eyes
i saw generations
of nations

people always find a way
they always build a door
swim an ocean
hold onto god
they always find a way
to survive
and speak about it after

now is not the time
to sit on the fence
when soldiers kill innocents
and call it self defence

ella zelensky

children care not
for other children's
different backgrounds
all they see is someone
they can be friends with
explore the world with
laugh endlessly with
hold hands with
someone they can love
the company of and
be excited to see

colour cannot
interfere with love

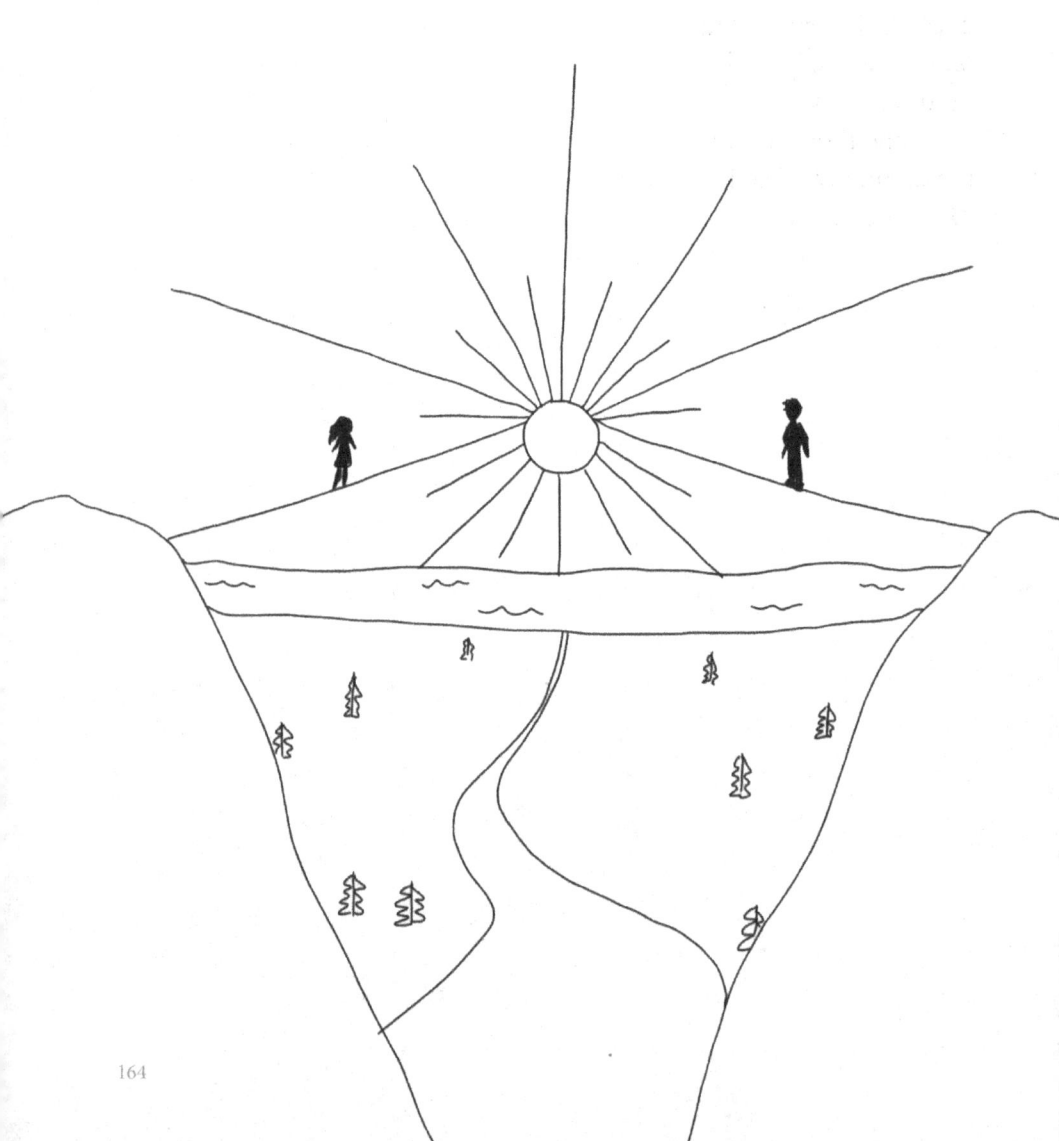

ella zelensky

remember the time
where we thought
the planets revolved
around the earth
we no longer believe this
for it was proven wrong
but nowadays we think the
world revolves around us
and human beings
so hate being proven wrong

at first light

the trees
are treated
as disposable
we invade
their land
like an army
driven by greed
holding sword
to neck
driving out all
the inhabitants

- deforestation

there are those who are unintentionally asleep
and those who choose to be
one is called misinformation
the other ideology

at first light

never evaluate someone
through a lens of violence
for the barrel of a gun
will only assume someone
as a target to be shot

ella zelensky

to be the future or to be history
that was humanity's most
intriguing mystery

at first light

we enjoy misconceptions
and barking them back
at those they're about
because toxicity and hate
feel good
humans enjoy the controversial
reinforcing their identity by
making no effort to understand
someone else's
is the equivalent of an
adrenaline rush
an intentional decision to
relish in the thrill of fear
because a humbling answer
is less exciting and
less self-serving than a
terrifying story

ella zelensky

solidarity isn't selective

at first light

in our outrage and
bitter hatred
we are too distracted
to notice that those
we curse and defame
are often more
happy
peaceful
and compassionate
than we are

ella zelensky

their eyes light up
as if they see something
the rest of the world
isn't developed enough
to see
and we say they are
from underdeveloped
countries

at first light

when you learn
more about those
around you
you realise you
were living in
your world
not the world

ella zelensky

him and his brother
sprinted up
and over the
hills together
as if their legs
wouldn't give in
as if they could
even fly

people said
what a performance
about the boy
but it wasn't quite
a performance
he has lived this reality
he isn't acting
he's re-enacting

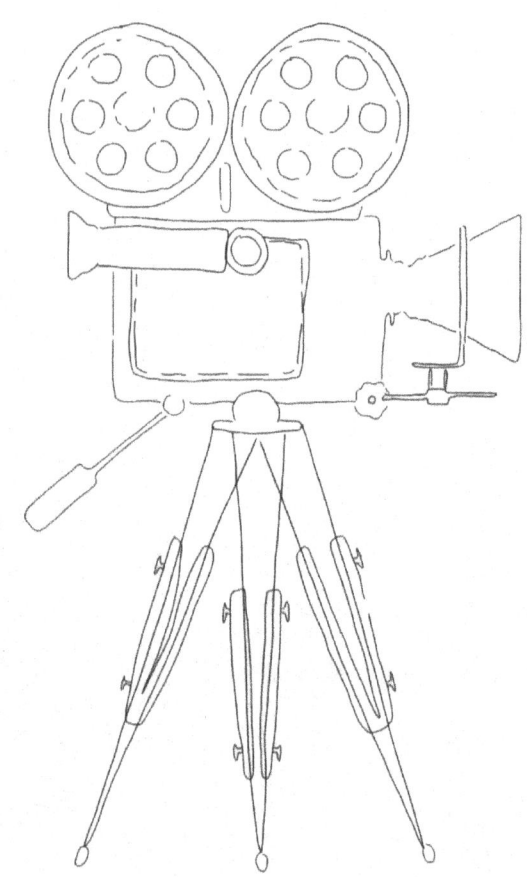

the butterflies ascended
in the field
golden hour illuminating
their flitting wings and
his melanin rich skin
he lifted his arms
to the sky and god
smiling

and still
we are capable of
world changing moments
who can deny the
human spirit then

ella zelensky

at first light

chapter five:
dreaming

we are only
a blink
in the universe
a twinkle
in time

ella zelensky

in a dream i saw
a kaleidoscope of people
in dresses swirling
the place into a spin
stars roared brighter than ever
and people sung generations
of emotions to life
as they danced my heart
joined in too
and i saw love
twinkling all around

    - the people i meet in my dreams

at first light

the seasons
turn and turn
like four children
dancing around
hand in hand infinitely

ella zelensky

i used to be a swimmer, and years underwater taught me things
years above water couldn't.
it taught me how to calm the heart. dismiss the noise.
to see under the surface. it taught me about survival during my depression.
diving into the water surrounded by bubbles and light had me lost
in a completely different world

at first light

what i envision
i wish i could
brush over
your eyes
and have you
see it too

    - butterfly hands

you say with pity
that i dream when
i am awake
but i would say
you are not
awake enough
to dream

at first light

the lantern spins so quickly
shapes flutter
like paper butterflies
across every wall
and in fleeting frames
i see memories not of my own
in motion from a past
both visually stunning
and frightening
it is a window only one sees
a conversation only
one side could confirm
and i wonder where
it is coming from

ella zelensky

the sand began to rise
as the two
travellers trudged
midway up the dune
staring at the sky
the sand formed
momentary pictures
floating ribbons
wavering and criss
crossing in and
out of form
quiet and in awe
amidst the flurry
their hearts believed
it to be one of the greatest
messages they had
ever seen in their lives

at first light

the mindscape
a beautiful realm is it not
filled with the intersection of
possible and impossible things

ella zelensky

it is a strange place
a realm caught
between life and death
with sunlight
bordering blindness
but just enough sight
to see a deeply hidden
forest no one can find
layers of colours flicker
and chimes ring when
the wind prompts them
and children chase
each other over logs
jumping like deer
in appearing and
disappearing wisps
of twinkling silver
i try to reach out to them
to follow where they are going
but the chimes ring once more
and i leave the place

at first light

trying to access memories
is like wandering
through a maze
and seeing people
who constantly appear
disappear and reappear
around the corner

ella zelensky

when i was young
i would wait
for my father
by the gate of
our balcony
he was dressed
in army uniform
done with his
day of work
my little fingers
would wrap
around the planks
eyes wide
with happiness
because my father
had come
he had come home
for me

at first light

we were his dream
and now we live it

ella zelensky

when i am deep in thought
and an idea occurs
the sparks go flying
the dominoes fall
and beautiful and
wonderful things
whir and whirl
in the room all around me
reflecting in my widening eyes
like a bright vision in the night

at first light

where did the deer
go when you
went to hunt it
only for you
to trip over logs
contemplate the arrow
and realise what was
stopping you was
saving someone else

ella zelensky

reflection or deflection
which will you choose

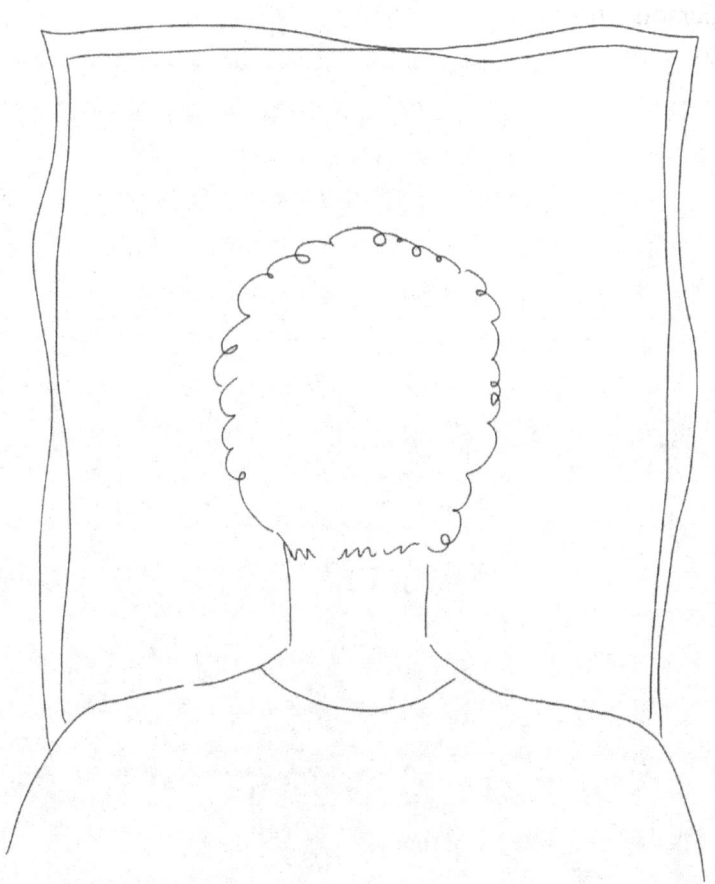

at first light

we find ourselves
in many escape
rooms in life
but hints cannot
always be given
to the person who
needs to learn

it often takes exploration
of the outside world
to make sense of our
inner world

at first light

cinema unites international audiences

many of our best ideas
emerge when we're not
trying to think of any
trust what the unknown
can reveal to you

at first light

i truly marvel
at butterflies
theirs is a brief life
and yet they fly to
such admirable heights
dancing together
in a flurry of celebration
under bright sunlight

now when i observe
my surroundings
there is never a shortage
of miracles to count

at first light

when everyone is asleep
you wake and traverse
the earth to feel the power
of god

thank you god for
not giving me
what i wanted
but what i needed

at first light

**it's risk but
it's necessity
it's fear
but it's time**

i am ready to be completely vulnerable
to where my fate will take me

at first light

at first light

your soulmate is waiting
for you to know
who you are before
you know who they are

ella zelensky

you are worthy
trust me
but trust yourself first
and foremost

at first light

be careful
the man who is
trying very hard
to sweep you
off your feet
is already aware you
have trouble
standing on them

your relationships
won't improve
unless you do

at first light

some people
keep taking the
love you give
them as a
test to gauge
how much love
you are willing
to give yourself

the wrong person
will make you
comfortable with
immature behaviour

appearance sells
but self-confidence tells

don't hold
onto someone
because of
your history
with them
when they don't
deserve a future
with you

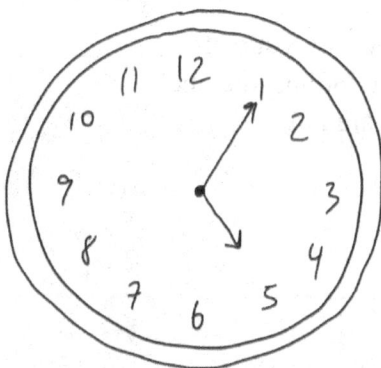

if you lose yourself
upon finding 'the one'
they are not

ella zelensky

falling out of someone's arms
and not into them
can be one of the most
important lessons on
dependency we can learn
it's a difficult fall
but it turns into a much
stronger rise

contentment
within oneself
decreases a desire
for the other

i am my own
before i am yours

you do not win a heart
like a trophy
you earn the heart
of the one who humbles you
in ways you didn't anticipate

if your burn for someone

assess whether it is out of
reciprocated love

or because they are
sacrificing your soul

at first light

**is respectful
courtship
not beautiful
anymore**

ella zelensky

when a door opens
you have the choice
to walk through it or close it

at first light

the moment
of over confession

one day
you will turn the corner
and find someone
who sets your heart ablaze
the person you very nearly
denied the existence of
will be the person whom
you will fall in love with
their presence will overcome you
and the chase will begin

we turn around
the wall
round by round
our hands
on it
always remaining
on the
other side
but waiting
for each other

it will be the long awaited reunion
the revealing of their name
where both recognise one another
as their twin flame

at first light

**god above us
decreed the space
between us**

at first light

i wear a long gown
of snow and flowers
knelt down in the garden
you find me and kneel
beside me too
we whisper conversation
to one another for
what feels like hours
until we both face our
heads neither away
nor towards one another
my eyebrows furrow
in anticipation of what
this moment may mean
and you suddenly rest
your head on mine slowly
something sacred arises
from the energy between us
it forms an invisible dome
around us in the garden
and i feel safe and full of
overflowing love beside you

when he saw her
outside with her friends
the next day
he noticed the flowers
he had gifted her
she had woven into
her hair

at first light

things and things
and things and things
fixed to wrapping
with cards fixed by strings
although it is beautiful
to receive many presents
it is the person
who gives them
it is the person's presence
that means the most

ella zelensky

he smiled to himself
and said
the lantern knows not
that she is a lantern

i know what it means
to hold someone tightly
because i know what
it feels like to be let go of

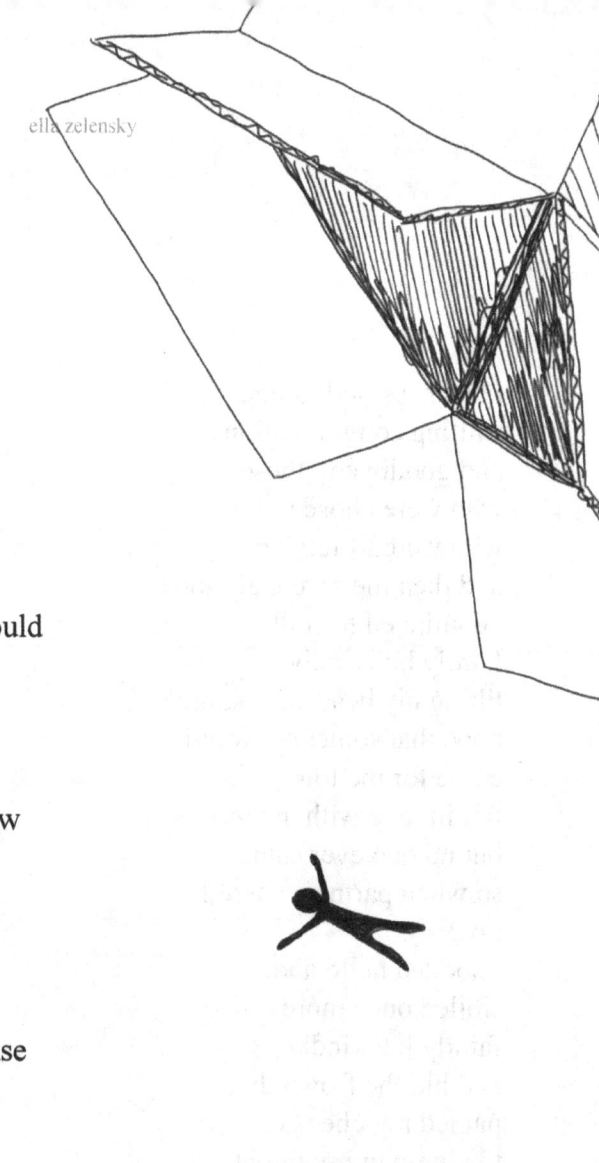

ella zelensky

they approached me when
the boys weren't around
and for a moment their
expression suggested they
were going to say
something nice
do you really think they would
ever like someone like you
they suddenly asked
your hopes are too high
you're different
just thought i'd let you know
and then they would leave
as the boys would arrive
and even though the boys
could see i was clearly
holding in something
i barely whispered a response
i barely called out the girls
who laughed at me
and they depended on that

i always stood in line
smiling congratulations
and goodbye to those
who were chosen
who weren't left last
and then they were all gone
i continued to smile
faintly but kindly
tilting my head with some
hope that someone would
come for me too
fall in love with me too
but no one ever came
so when partners passed
my way
i nodded hello and
smiled once more
faintly but kindly
and hid the frown that
pained my cheeks
the lump in my throat
the shimmer in my eyes
the fear that perhaps
men might come my way
but pass me for another
instead

ella zelensky

maybe one day
a man will spot me on
those steps
and sit with me too
not out of pity
but out of love

at first light

i want my whole
being to be sure
that i love someone
and they love me

ella zelensky

i will not be the embarrassment
of the one who will love me

at first light

her eyes were
always open
but he was
the one who
helped her see

ella zelensky

as the light of dawn
set her eyes aglow
he found himself
astonished that he
hadn't realised his
desire to love her
so long ago

at first light

our eyes stare
into one another
so intensely
reality trips
and i can no longer
tell whether i am
looking through
my eyes or yours

- connection

if i miss you
i need only
remember you

i am learning to
not fear the girl
who waited quietly
on those steps
to believe that someday
someone will
stay behind
look me in
the eyes
and take my hand
as they tell me to rise

ella zelensky

i place the flower
in the water
with all the sadness
i once carried
and watch as it
flows downstream
today
i tell myself
i am worthy
today
i tell myself
that someone will appear
before i doubt
his existence
and will love me
in the ways i
always dreamed of

i dance through
the chambers
of my heart

ella zelensky

at first light

the concluding word

at first light

I didn't remember saying to my mother as a child that I wanted to become an author. At first I was an artist, always drawing my way through life. That was how people knew me. But when grade eight came along, the drawing stopped. My heart did too. The depression from the bullying was something I couldn't prepare for, and even my creativity couldn't flourish its way through, at least for a little while. I used to call the writing a mistake, because I hid myself in the library one day and decided to randomly write down my feelings. Now I understand that 'mistake' is the wrong word. One journal entry turned into another and another until I realised that the poetry was always hidden inside of me. The realisation just hadn't hit until that point. Since then it has changed my life, as I hope it has changed others' lives.

Creative people are often ridiculed or treated differently growing up, particularly in school. At first we are asked to unapologetically tap into and express our creativity as kids. As we grow older however, we are suddenly asked to stay away from it unless we want our grades to drop. By this point, the mixed signals are not only confusing but frightening to us. Because now, creativity is made synonymous with present and future failure. It is linked to being 'wrong', and no one likes being put in that box. This mentality is incomprehensible in a world full of creativity and thus innovation. As Ken Robinson said: "if you're not prepared to be wrong, you will never come up with anything original".

Over the years I've had people say they wish they could be creative or write poetically, and my response is always this – you are and always will be creative, but certain environments have likely tried to condition it out of you. It saddens me deeply that something as beautiful and honest as creativity has been refashioned into something a large segment of the world population genuinely fears. It's like fearing love. Love isn't inherently bad or dangerous, it is simply those who are of ill intention who warp its essence. Like love, creativity is supposed be filled with warmth and welcome and celebration. It is not something to be feared. I want my work to inspire people to write. Every person's emotion, experience and honesty will produce work far more astonishing than they allow themselves to believe.

The poet shouldn't be seen as a teacher. That would be dishonest. The poet is also the one who is taught. I do not write to teach, I write to inspire collective reflection. I too am among the audience. Many of these poems come from hard lessons I have aspired to understand and embrace by the wisdom of those around me. Thank you for humbling me with it, and for continuing to. Poetry would not be what it is if we didn't reinforce that in the end, we are all in this together. We are equal.

Honour your creativity and look for the excitement in what is to come in your life journey. You are allowed to celebrate both.

About the Author

Ella is a mixed race Australian published author and current university student at the University of QLD, majoring in anthropology, and with interests also in Religion, Language, Cross Cultural Communication and Film and Television.

Since she was young, culture, race, religion, language, cinematography, and activism have played a significant role in her creative work and academic studies.

After struggling with fitting in during her early high school years, writing poetry helped her cope and rise above. Writing eventually became serious to her and she began sharing her work on her social media platform.

Ella published her first poetry book, Little Dreamer in March of 2021 and her second book Divine Decree in January 2022.

Her dream to be a humanitarian worker, as well as interests in education, mental health and equality inspire many of her poems and quotes. Through Ella's passion for people, reform, and harmony, she wishes to help others own their identity, take a stand, forgive, unite, and ultimately heal.

In 2018 Ella launched The Leadlight Project, as a creative hub for teens struggling with social isolation and loneliness. The Projects aim, to gather identified teens to develop and create artwork, poetry, short films, and photography to be showcased and celebrated at a collaborative exhibition, scheduled for the 12th of October 2019, in conjunction with QLD Mental Health. Unfortunately, due to ongoing illness, Ella had to place the Project's collaborative Exhibitions on hold. In 2021, the re-formatted project relaunched via a new Shopfront whereby a percentage of sales will be donated to children's charities dear to Ella's heart, including Unicef's Yemen Crisis.

www.ellazelensky.com

At First Light ISBN: 978-0-6450978-6-3
At First Light e-book ISBN: 978-0-6450978-7-0

© Ella Zelensky, 2023. All rights reserved

notes

www.ingramcontent.com/pod-product-compliance
Lightning Source LLC
Chambersburg PA
CBHW011149290426
44109CB00025B/2548